# The ABCs of Honey Bees

Written by
## Nina Elizondo
Blue Water Bee Publishing

*To Mr. Hodgie Holgerson for teaching me everything I know about beekeeping.*

The ABCs of Honey Bees by Nina Elizondo

www.bluewaterbee.com

Copyright ©2017 Blue Water Bee Publishing LLC

All rights reserved. This book or parts thereof may not be reproduced in any form by any means - electronic, mechanical, photocopy, recording, or otherwise - without prior written permission of the publisher, except as provided by United States of America copyright law. For permissions, contact the author at www.bluewaterbee.com.

ISBN 978-0-9997293-1-1

Library of Congress Control Number 2018937445

A is for Apiary. An apiary is a honey bee farm that can have a few to many bee hives. The number of hives you can put in an apiary depends on the resources of pollen and nectar nearby. Honey bees need pollen and nectar to make food. Pollen provides the bees with the protein they need and the nectar provides the carbohydrates.

Honey Bee    Carpenter Bee    Mason Bee    Bumble bee

B is for Bee. There are many types of bees like the carpenter bee, bumble bee, mason bee, and of course the honey bee. One of the most well-known species of honey bees is the *Apis mellifera,* or European Honey Bee, which is the type most kept by people to make honey.

C is for Corbicula. The corbicula is the honey bee's pollen basket on its hind legs. The honey bee pushes the pollen to the basket. The hairs around the basket keep the pollen in while the bee flies back to the hive.

Corbicula

Drone     Queen     Worker

**D** is for Drone. The drone bee is one of the three types of honey bees you will find in a honey bee hive. They are always males and cannot sting you. Their main job is to mate with a queen bee. In winter, drones are kicked out of the hive since they do not have a job to do.

E is for Equipment. Beekeepers use different equipment for different reasons, either to protect themselves from the bees or to help them in the hives. They use a veil to protect their faces and gloves to protect their hands so the bees cannot sting them. The smoker stops the bees' communication because it masks their pheromones with the smoke. Beekeepers use the hive tool to make it easier to pry the frames apart to inspect the hive and make sure it is healthy.

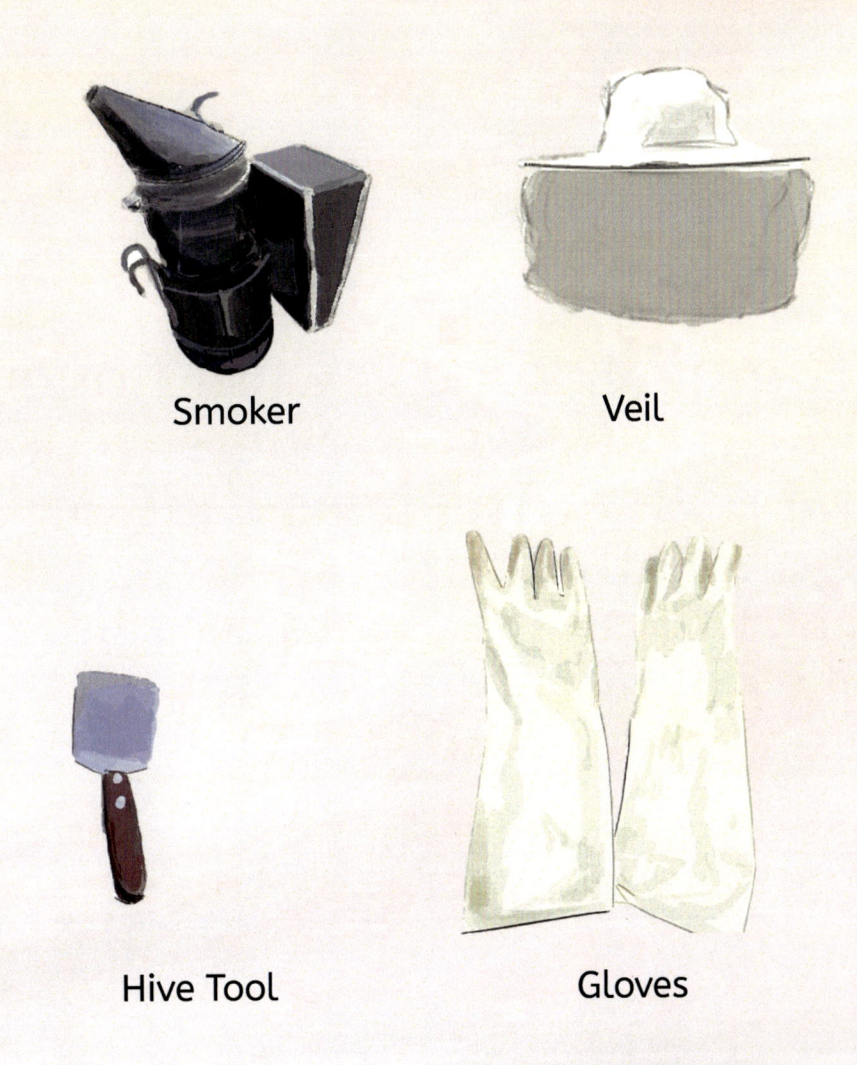

Smoker

Veil

Hive Tool

Gloves

F is for Forage. Forage is what honey bees do when they visit flowers to get nectar and pollen. The bees that do this work are called forager bees. When honey bees forage they stay within a three-mile radius and they only forage from one type of plant at a time.

Wax

**G** is for Glands. Honey bees have glands all over their bodies that help them communicate with each other and to make resources to help with the hive. They have glands in their heads that make royal jelly to feed the queen and the young brood. Sometimes you can see honey bees sticking their bottoms into the air. They are releasing pheromones from the gland at the end of their abdomen that helps other bees find the hive. Honey bees have glands on their abdomen that make wax for the comb.

H is for Honey. A honey bee only makes five drops of honey in her entire life. When the bees store the honey, they store it in cells in the comb and cap it to preserve the honey until they are ready to eat it. Honey can be used in many ways. Most people use honey as a sweetener. It can be used for medical reasons too. It can help heal wounds and can fight infections because it kills bacteria. Pure honey will never spoil.

Frame of capped and uncapped honey

Honey Pot

Antenna
Head
Thorax
Leg
Wing
Abdomen

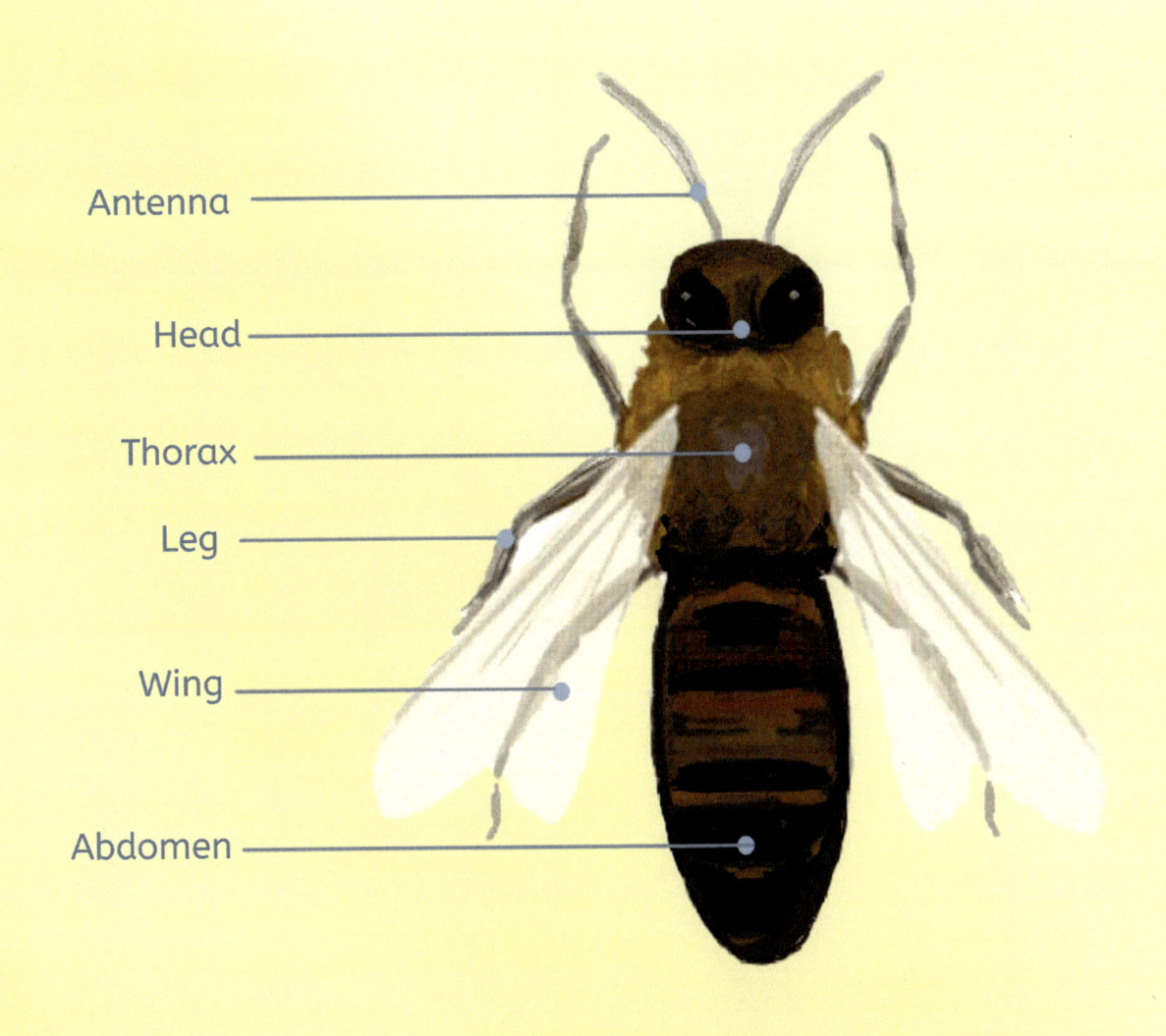

**I** is for Insect. All insects have certain properties in common. They all have a head, an abdomen, and a thorax. They also have two antennae, four wings, and six legs. In addition to the honey bee, ants, hornets, and wasps are insects.

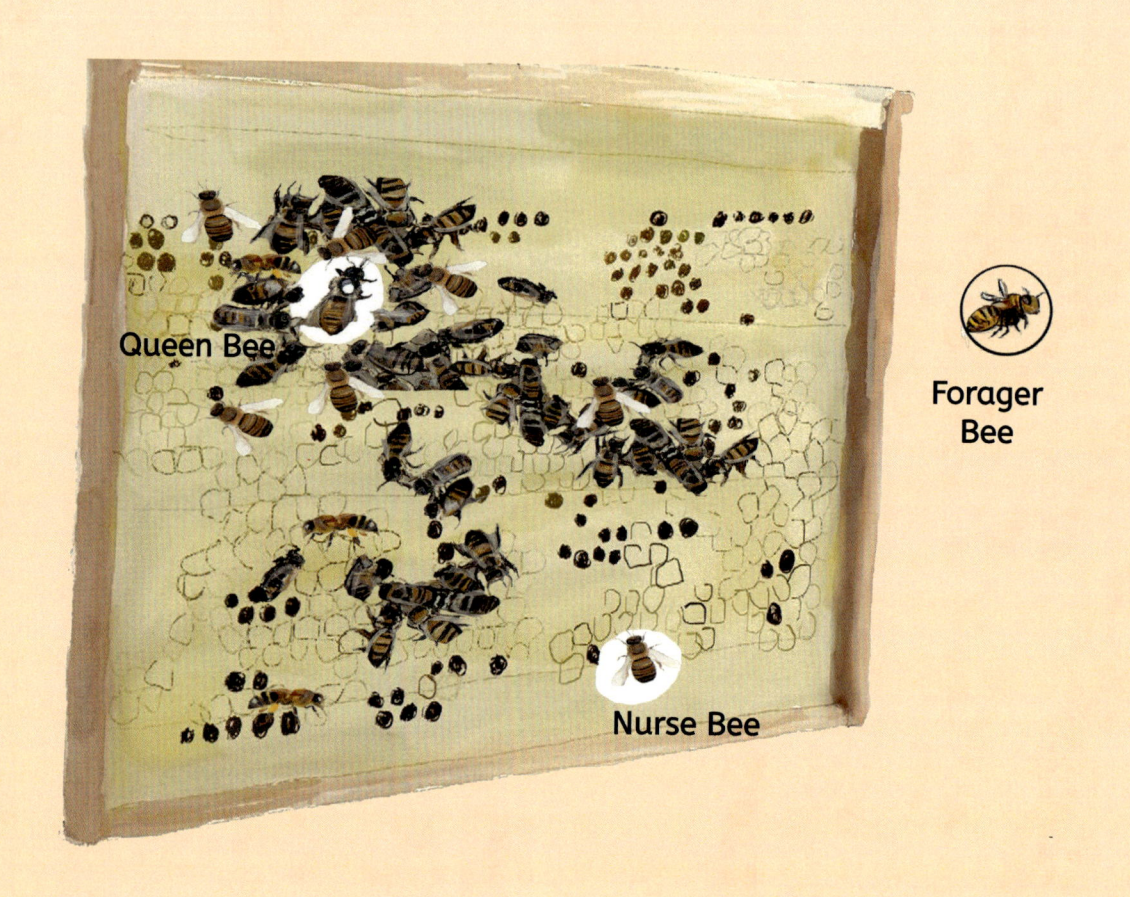

**J** is for Jobs. There are lots of jobs in the hive and outside. There are nurse bees who clean the hive, feed the brood, and take care of the queen. There is also the queen who lays eggs to keep the hive going because worker bees only live six weeks during the busy season which is spring and summer. Finally, forager bees collect nectar and pollen from flowers and bring it back to the hive.

K is for Keeping. When people keep honey bees, they keep them in a hive. There are two different types of hives normally used. The Langstroth hive is the most commonly used hive and it is made of boxes stacked on each other. In this type of hive, you give the bees the foundation in the frames on which to build their comb. The other type of hive is the Top Bar hive, which is a long, trapezoidal-shaped box. The bars of this hive do not have foundation and the bees have to build all of their own comb.

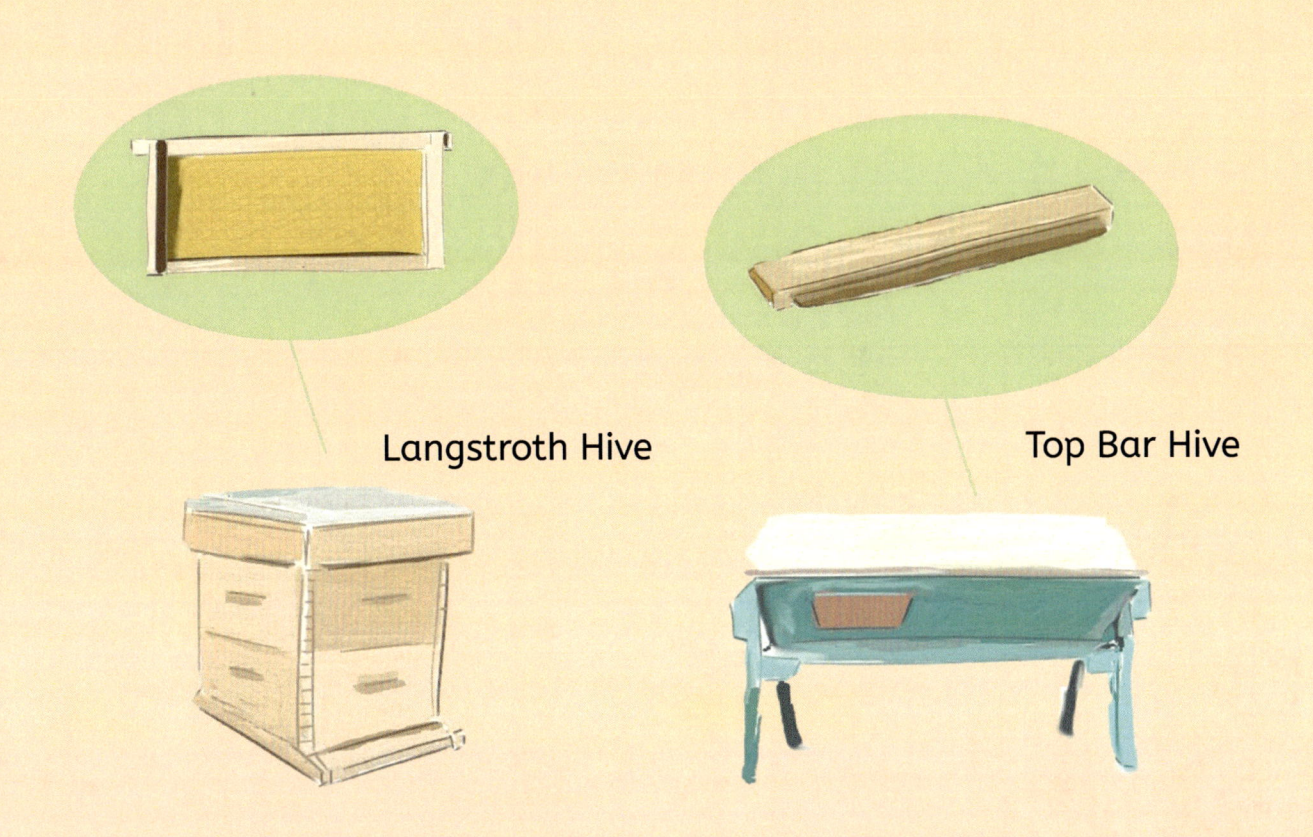

Langstroth Hive

Top Bar Hive

Egg   LARVA   Pre-Pupa Larva (With Cell Cap)   PUPA   Adult

L is for Lifecycle. The life cycle of the honey bee contains four stages: Egg, Larva, Pupa, and Adult. The egg stage lasts for three days and then they hatch into larvae. Larvae are fed royal jelly for the first four days of the larva stage, then their diets are switched to bee's bread, which is a mixture of pollen and honey. If it is a queen larva, her diet will not switch and she will remain on a strict diet of royal jelly. Right before the bees go into the pupa stage, the bees cap the larva's cell with wax. In the cell, the bee transforms into a pupa and then emerges from the cell as an adult bee. The time lapse from the egg to the adult stage is different depending on whether it is a worker, drone or queen bee.

**M** is for Melittology. Melittology is the scientific study of bees. Melittologists study many species of bees, not just the honey bee, including bumble bees, mason bees, and resin bees. Scientists can study new species of bees, foraging behavior, and a bee's nesting environment.

N is for Nectar. Nectar is the sweet liquid that bees get from the flowers. The forager bees carry the nectar back to the hive and pass it on to the house bees. While the bees are passing the nectar around, enzymes are added to it from the bee's gut. Then the bee stores it in a honeycomb cell. The bees fan the nectar to evaporate the water which ripens into honey and then they put a cap on it to save it for later.

O is for Old. Beekeeping has been around for 5,000 years. We have hieroglyphics and clay sculptures that show ancient Egyptians keeping bees. Honey bees were important because the ancient Egyptians thought the honey bee came from the sun god which made it a sacred insect. They were also important to the Egyptians because their honey was used for medicine and used to sweeten foods.

Stigma

Anther

**P** is for Pollination. This occurs when the bee transfers pollen from the anthers of a flower to the stigma of another flower it visits while foraging. This allows the plant to bear fruit.

Q is for Queen. The queen is the only bee that lays eggs in the hive unless she is sick or gone. Queen bees can live up to five years. To make it easier to locate her and to know how old a queen is, some beekeepers mark her with a special color-coded dot. The queen bee is the only honey bee that can sting more than once because she has a smooth stinger instead of a barbed one. She uses her stinger to kill rival queens.

Larva in royal jelly

R is for Royal Jelly. The worker bees secrete this white jelly from the glands in their head. All larvae receive royal jelly for the first four days of their lives. After that, only larvae that will become queens continue to receive royal jelly for food. This is the only food she eats once she starts laying eggs. People use royal jelly for healing purposes.

S is for Swarm. When the bees start to outgrow their hive, they build new queen cells for a new queen to be born (the cells look like a peanut). The honey bees put the queen on a diet so she will be able to fly away with about half of the colony's bees. They usually land on a tree branch until the scout bees can find a permanent home. After the swarm is gone, the new queens in the original colony hatch from their cells and battle to see who will be the new queen since only one can live in the hive.

T is for Threat. Honey bee populations have been declining. Pests like the varroa mite, hive beetle and wax moth are threats to the honey bee that affect the health of the bees or causes destruction in the hive. Pesticides, which are chemicals sprayed on crops to kill pests, act like poison to the bees. Colony Collapse Disorder (CCD) is another threat to the honey bee population that happens when most of the worker bees leave the hive while the queen and a few young bees are left behind and eventually die. Scientists do not know the exact reason for CCD.

**U** is for Ultraviolet (UV) light. This is a special type of light that helps honey bees and other pollinators find flowers for foraging. The UV light makes a color pattern on the flower for the insects that guides them to where the pollen and nectar are.

Venom Sac

Stinger

V is for Venom. Honey bees have venom that comes out of their stingers when they sting you. Even without the bee attached to it, the venom sac will continue to pump venom so it is important to scrape the sac and stinger out of your skin.

W is for Worker Bee. The worker bees do many jobs for the hive. They forage for food, they clean the hive, they fan and cap the honey, feed and care for the brood and they attend to the queen. All worker bees are female and will only lay eggs if the queen is unable to.

Foraging

Cleaning Hive

Caring for Brood

**X** is for X-ray. Scientists use micro X-rays, or three-dimensional X-rays, to study honey bees' bodies and hives. By X-raying the honey bee's brain, scientists can see how they might learn and memorize. The X-rays can help scientists look into a bee hive without disturbing it. This information gives scientists a better understanding of the bee colony, threats to the colony and better ways to manage the hive.

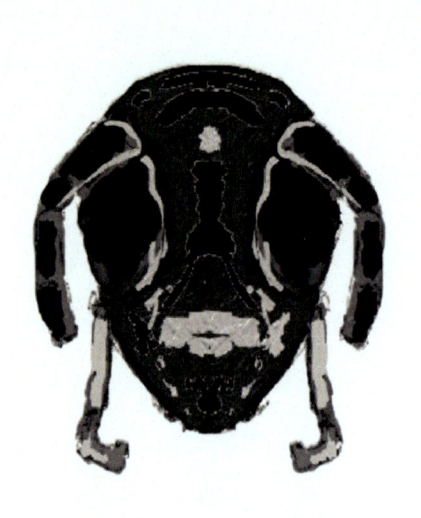

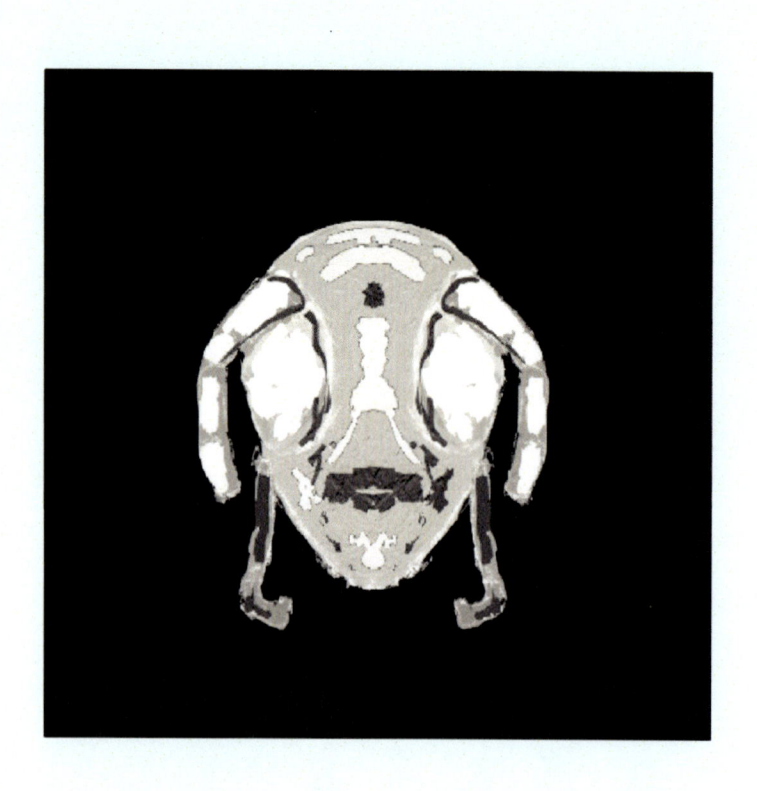

**Y** is for Years. A queen bee can live up to five years. To know how old a queen is, beekeepers mark the queen with a color that represents the year in which she was born. There are five colors: White, Yellow, Red, Green and Blue. A beekeeper will mark a queen bee with white if she is born in a year that ends with a 1 or 6. It is the same process with the other four colors. Beekeepers have created a saying to help them remember the sequence of colors: Will You Raise Good Bees (White Yellow Red Green Blue).

*Year Ending In:*

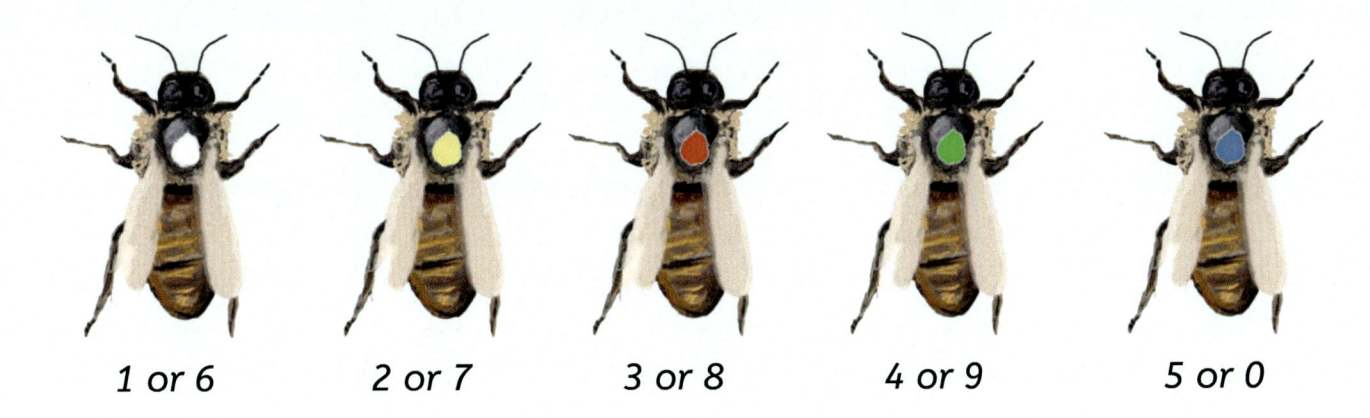

| 1 or 6 | 2 or 7 | 3 or 8 | 4 or 9 | 5 or 0 |

**Z** is for Zigzag. Zigzag describes the pattern the honey bee makes when it does the Waggle Dance. This dance is a communication method to tell the other bees where to forage for pollen and nectar when the distance is far from the hive. The bee runs in the shape of a figure-eight, and does the zigzag or waggle pattern, when it cuts across the circle. How long the bee waggles communicates the distance of the foraging area and the direction the bee waggles in tells other bees where it is located in relation to the sun. The bees do the Round Dance when the foraging is closer to the hive.

## ABOUT THE AUTHOR

Nina started beekeeping at nine-years old after learning how interesting honey bees are from her 4H club. Since then, she has learned even more about honey bees and their world. She started keeping bees in a Top Bar hive and then earned her Langstroth hive through her 4H club. Nina earned the Most Valuable Beekeeper Award in 2017 for her work in the 4H club as well as earning third place for her beeswax in the Virginia State Fair. She enjoys art and baking in her free time. You can read more about her journey to becoming a beekeeper and everything in between at www.bluewaterbee.com.

Made in the USA
Lexington, KY
27 July 2018